Affirmations
TO HELP YOU
Really Move On

PIERRE ALEX JEANTY

Copyright © 2021 by Pierre Alex Jeanty

All rights reserved. No part of this publication may be reproduced, stored in a retrieval system, or transmitted in any form or by any means – electronic, mechanical, photocopying, recording, or otherwise – without the written permission of the publisher.

Cover Design & Layout: Patti Jefferson

ISBN-13: 978-1-949191-17-2

For more information, please visit:
pierrejeanty.com

Schools & Businesses

Jeanius Publishing books are available at quantity discounts with bulk purchases.

For more information, please email
contact@jeaniuspublishing.com

Affirmations TO HELP YOU Really Move On

jeanius PUBLISHING

Let me start by saying that I am extremely proud of you! Your pursuit for growth and recovery is commendable and beautiful. I want to not only acknowledge that but also cheer you on. You will get to the other side, you will conquer, you will succeed.

In order for this exercise to achieve its purpose, you have to commit, put in the necessary effort, and stay consistent. Block out time in your day to do these affirmations. Say them out loud - however many times you need to. Memorize them and recite them in the mirror if it helps you. Do whatever it takes to make these words real to you. This is what will help them come to life.

Please also do the writing portion of it. Writing is another way to help you believe those words. Write the affirmations in the space we have for it. Write more in a journal if you need to.

Also dive into the thought exercise. They are meant to help you really go deep and reflect. Be honest in your answers. They may not be pretty or easy but you owe yourself that truth so you can really move on.

Now that you are ready, let's embark on this journey. I am right there with you. You can do it.

WEEK 1
"I will not..."

Say these affirmations aloud every day.

I will not
let the bad shape me.

I will not
let the hurt mold me.

I will not
let the pain change me.

I will not
let the heartbreak break me.

I will not be a victim.
I am a victor who conquers
everything meant to take me down.

Write one of the affirmations each night before bed.

Day

1 _____
_____

2 _____
_____

3 _____
_____

4 _____
_____

5 _____
_____

6 _____
_____

7 _____
_____

THOUGHT 💡 EXERCISE

Day 1: What are your goals for starting this healing journey?

_____
_____
_____
_____

Day 2: Which affirmation speaks loudest to you? Why?

_____
_____
_____
_____

Day 3: In what ways have you already focused on that one?

_____
_____
_____
_____

Day 4: Which affirmation is your biggest challenge? Why?

_____

_____

_____

Day 5: What can you do to make it easier to believe?

_____

_____

_____

Day 6: How do you feel about these affirmations now?

_____

_____

Day 7: Write your own "I will not..." affirmation.

_____

_____

WEEK 2

"I am free..."

Say these affirmations aloud every day.

I am free
of emotional attachment to people
that are part of my past.

I am free
from a mentally-draining
experience.

I am free
from an unfruitful relationship.

I am free
to move forward to the
better that awaits me.

Write one of the affirmations each night before bed.

Day 1 — SAT 11/2 — I am FREE of Emotional attachment to people that are part of my past.

2

3

4

5

6

7

THOUGHT EXERCISE

Day 1: What does freedom mean to you in this case?

_____

_____

_____

_____

Day 2: Which affirmation speaks loudest to you? Why?

_____

_____

_____

_____

Day 3: In what ways have you already focused on that one?

_____

_____

_____

_____

Day 4: Which affirmation is your biggest challenge? Why?

_____

_____

_____

Day 5: What can you do to make it easier to believe?

_____

_____

_____

Day 6: How do you feel about these affirmations now?

_____

_____

_____

Day 7: Write your own "I am free…" affirmation.

_____

_____

WEEK 3

"I am committed..."

Say these affirmations aloud every day.

I am committed to my healing.

I am committed to my progress.

I am committed to my self-love.

I am committed to my self-care.

I am committed to my mental, spiritual and physical health.

I am committed to being better, happier, and stronger.

Write one of the affirmations each night before bed.

Day
1 _____
  _____

2 _____
  _____

3 _____
  _____

4 _____
  _____

5 _____
  _____

6 _____
  _____

7 _____
  _____

THOUGHT EXERCISE

Day 1: What does commitment mean to you in this case?

_____

_____

_____

_____

Day 2: Which affirmation speaks loudest to you? Why?

_____

_____

_____

_____

Day 3: In what ways have you already focused on that one?

_____

_____

_____

_____

Day 4: Which affirmation is your biggest challenge? Why?

_____

_____

_____

_____

Day 5: What can you do to make it easier to believe?

_____

_____

_____

Day 6: How do you feel about these affirmations now?

_____

_____

Day 7: Write your own "I am committed..." affirmation.

_____

_____

WEEK 4

"I will no longer..."

Say these affirmations aloud every day.

I will no longer leave
my heart in the wrong hands.

I will no longer give
other people the key to my
happiness.

I will no longer love
anyone else before I love myself.

I will no longer chase
relationships until I am ready.

I will no longer sacrifice myself
to gain anything from anyone else.

Write one of the affirmations each night before bed.

Day

1
_____
_____

2
_____
_____

3
_____
_____

4
_____
_____

5
_____
_____

6
_____
_____

7
_____
_____

THOUGHT EXERCISE

Day 1: How do you feel about holding yourself accountable?

_____
_____
_____

Day 2: Which affirmation speaks loudest to you? Why?

_____
_____
_____

Day 3: In what ways have you already focused on that one?

_____
_____
_____

Day 4: Which affirmation is your biggest challenge? Why?

_____

_____

_____

Day 5: What can you do to make it easier to believe?

_____

_____

_____

Day 6: How do you feel about these affirmations now?

_____

_____

_____

Day 7: Write your own "I will no longer..." affirmation.

_____

_____

WEEK 5

"Today I choose..."

Say these affirmations aloud every day.

Today I choose
my own love.

Today I choose
my confidence.

Today I choose
my own path.

Today I choose
the things I value.

Today I choose
the person in the mirror.

Write one of the affirmations each night before bed.

Day

1 _____
_____

2 _____
_____

3 _____
_____

4 _____
_____

5 _____
_____

6 _____
_____

7 _____
_____

THOUGHT EXERCISE

Day 1: How do you feel about taking control (choosing)?

_____

_____

_____

Day 2: Which affirmation speaks loudest to you? Why?

_____

_____

_____

Day 3: In what ways have you already focused on that one?

_____

_____

_____

Day 4: Which affirmation is your biggest challenge? Why?

_____

_____

_____

Day 5: What can you do to make it easier to believe?

_____

_____

_____

Day 6: How do you feel about these affirmations now?

_____

_____

_____

Day 7: Write your own "Today I choose…" affirmation.

_____

_____

WEEK 6

"I release..."

Say these affirmations aloud every day.

I release my hunger
for revenge.

I release my anger
against those who've hurt me.

I release the hurt
that is still inside me.

I release the things trying
to badly influence my good heart.

I release everything
that is holding me back.

Write one of the affirmations each night before bed.

Day

1 _____
  _____

2 _____
  _____

3 _____
  _____

4 _____
  _____

5 _____
  _____

6 _____
  _____

7 _____
  _____

THOUGHT EXERCISE

Day 1: What does release mean to you in this case?

_____

_____

_____

_____

Day 2: Which affirmation speaks loudest to you? Why?

_____

_____

_____

_____

Day 3: In what ways have you already focused on that one?

_____

_____

_____

_____

Day 4: Which affirmation is your biggest challenge? Why?

_____

_____

_____

_____

Day 5: What can you do to make it easier to believe?

_____

_____

_____

_____

Day 6: How do you feel about these affirmations now?

_____

_____

_____

Day 7: Write your own "I release…" affirmation.

_____

_____

WEEK 7

"I am brave..."

Say these affirmations aloud every day.

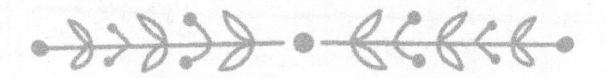

I am brave for leaving
what was no longer healthy.

I am brave for choosing
me even if it means being alone.

I am brave for forgiving
those that hurt me.

I am brave for choosing
peace over chaos.

I am brave for demanding
more than the minimum.

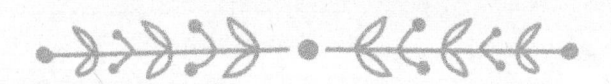

Write one of the affirmations each night before bed.

Day

1 _____

2 _____

3 _____

4 _____

5 _____

6 _____

7 _____

THOUGHT EXERCISE

Day 1: What does bravery mean to you in this case?

_____

_____

_____

_____

Day 2: Which affirmation speaks loudest to you? Why?

_____

_____

_____

_____

Day 3: In what ways have you already focused on that one?

_____

_____

_____

_____

Day 4: Which affirmation is your biggest challenge? Why?

_____

_____

_____

Day 5: What can you do to make it easier to believe?

_____

_____

_____

Day 6: How do you feel about these affirmations now?

_____

_____

_____

Day 7: Write your own "I am brave..." affirmation.

_____

_____

WEEK 8

"I accept..."

Say these affirmations aloud every day.

I accept help
from those who care for me.

I accept the support
of those who love me.

I accept the helping hands
of those who appreciate me.

I accept I cannot
do everything alone.

I accept I need
to let the ones placed in my life
be active in my life.

Write one of the affirmations each night before bed.

Day

1 _____
_____

2 _____
_____

3 _____
_____

4 _____
_____

5 _____
_____

6 _____
_____

7 _____
_____

THOUGHT EXERCISE

Day 1: What does acceptance mean to you in this case?

_____

_____

_____

_____

Day 2: Which affirmation speaks loudest to you? Why?

_____

_____

_____

_____

Day 3: In what ways have you already focused on that one?

_____

_____

_____

_____

Day 4: Which affirmation is your biggest challenge? Why?

_____
_____
_____
_____

Day 5: What can you do to make it easier to believe?

_____
_____
_____
_____

Day 6: How do you feel about these affirmations now?

_____
_____
_____

Day 7: Write your own "I accept…" affirmation.

_____
_____

WEEK 9

"I am..."

Say these affirmations aloud every day.

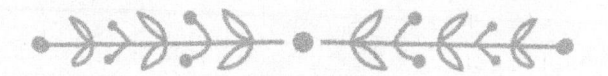

I am gentle
with myself.

I am loyal
to my needs.

I am grateful
for my present.

I am forgiving
of my past.

I am happy
to be the person I am now
and will become.

Write one of the affirmations each night before bed.

Day

1 _____

2 _____

3 _____

4 _____

5 _____

6 _____

7 _____

THOUGHT EXERCISE

Day 1: How do you currently see yourself?

_____
_____
_____

Day 2: Which affirmation speaks loudest to you? Why?

_____
_____
_____

Day 3: In what ways have you already focused on that one?

_____
_____
_____

Day 4: Which affirmation is your biggest challenge? Why?

_____

_____

_____

_____

Day 5: What can you do to make it easier to believe?

_____

_____

_____

_____

Day 6: How do you feel about these affirmations now?

_____

_____

_____

_____

Day 7: Write your own "I am..." affirmation.

_____

_____

WEEK 10
"I am strong enough..."

Say these affirmations aloud every day.

I am strong enough
to defeat my moments of
loneliness.

I am strong enough
to overcome my moments of
weakness.

I am strong enough
to defeat my misleading desires.

I am strong enough
to wait until I am truly ready
and right.

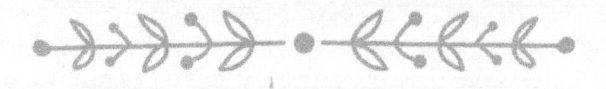

Write one of the affirmations each night before bed.

Day

1 _____

2 _____

3 _____

4 _____

5 _____

6 _____

7 _____

THOUGHT EXERCISE

Day 1: What does strength mean to you in this case?

_____

_____

_____

_____

Day 2: Which affirmation speaks loudest to you? Why?

_____

_____

_____

_____

Day 3: In what ways have you already focused on that one?

_____

_____

_____

_____

Day 4: Which affirmation is your biggest challenge? Why?

_____

_____

_____

_____

Day 5: What can you do to make it easier to believe?

_____

_____

_____

_____

Day 6: How do you feel about these affirmations now?

_____

_____

_____

Day 7: Write your own "I am strong..." affirmation.

_____

_____

WEEK 11

"I own up to..."

Say these affirmations aloud every day.

I own up to
my past bad choices and
foolish decisions.

I own up to my unwise actions.

I own up to
my impulsive reactions.

I own up to
my self-inflicted pain.

I own up to my responsibilities
because when I do I reflect honestly
and grow

Write one of the affirmations each night before bed.

Day

1 _____

2 _____

3 _____

4 _____

5 _____

6 _____

7 _____

THOUGHT EXERCISE

Day 1: What does "own up" mean to you in this case?

_____

_____

_____

Day 2: Which affirmation speaks loudest to you? Why?

_____

_____

_____

Day 3: In what ways have you already focused on that one?

_____

_____

_____

Day 4: Which affirmation is your biggest challenge? Why?

_____

_____

_____

Day 5: What can you do to make it easier to believe?

_____

_____

_____

Day 6: How do you feel about these affirmations now?

_____

_____

_____

Day 7: Write your own "I own up to..." affirmation.

_____

_____

WEEK 12

"I forgive..."

Say these affirmations aloud every day.

I forgive the people
who used me and betrayed me.

I forgive the people
who see only the worse in me.

I forgive the people
who gossip about me and speak
down on me.

I forgive the people
who were committed to
misunderstanding me.

I forgive myself.

Write one of the affirmations each night before bed.

Day

1

2

3

4

5

6

7

THOUGHT EXERCISE

Day 1: What does forgiveness mean to you in this case?

_____

_____

_____

_____

Day 2: Which affirmation speaks loudest to you? Why?

_____

_____

_____

_____

Day 3: In what ways have you already focused on that one?

_____

_____

_____

_____

Day 4: Which affirmation is your biggest challenge? Why?

_____
_____
_____
_____

Day 5: What can you do to make it easier to believe?

_____
_____
_____
_____

Day 6: How do you feel about these affirmations now?

_____
_____
_____

Day 7: Write your own "I forgive…" affirmation.

_____
_____

WEEK 13

"I am allowed..."

Say these affirmations aloud every day.

I am allowed
to say no or not right now.

I am allowed
to reject what I don't need.

I am allowed
to say I am working on me.

I am allowed
to say I am still afraid.

I am allow to choose for myself
without feeling guilty.

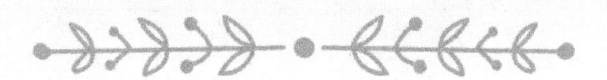

Write one of the affirmations each night before bed.

Day

1 _____

2 _____

3 _____

4 _____

5 _____

6 _____

7 _____

THOUGHT EXERCISE

Day 1: How does allowing yourself these things make you feel?

_____
_____
_____
_____

Day 2: Which affirmation speaks loudest to you? Why?

_____
_____
_____
_____

Day 3: In what ways have you already focused on that one?

_____
_____
_____
_____

Day 4: Which affirmation is your biggest challenge? Why?

_____

_____

_____

Day 5: What can you do to make it easier to believe?

_____

_____

_____

Day 6: How do you feel about these affirmations now?

_____

_____

_____

Day 7: Write your own "I am allowed…" affirmation.

_____

_____

WEEK 14

"I will ... again."

Say these affirmations aloud every day.

I will
trust again.

I will
learn to be vulnerable again.

I will give myself
to a relationship again.

I will believe
in love again.

I will give love
and accept love again.

Write one of the affirmations each night before bed.

Day

1 _____
_____

2 _____
_____

3 _____
_____

4 _____
_____

5 _____
_____

6 _____
_____

7 _____
_____

THOUGHT EXERCISE

Day 1: What does being healed in the future look like for you?

_____
_____
_____
_____

Day 2: Which affirmation speaks loudest to you? Why?

_____
_____
_____
_____

Day 3: In what ways have you already focused on that one?

_____
_____
_____
_____

Day 4: Which affirmation is your biggest challenge? Why?

_____
_____
_____
_____

Day 5: What can you do to make it easier to believe?

_____
_____
_____
_____

Day 6: How do you feel about these affirmations now?

_____
_____
_____

Day 7: Write your own "I will... again." affirmation.

_____
_____

WEEK 15

"I believe I am..."

Say these affirmations aloud every day.

I believe I am
healed and whole.

I believe I am
worthy.

I believe I am
loved and appreciated.

I believe I am
valuable.

I believe I am
enough.

Write one of the affirmations each night before bed.

Day

1 _____

2 _____

3 _____

4 _____

5 _____

6 _____

7 _____

THOUGHT EXERCISE

Day 1: Is it easy or difficult to believe in yourself? Why?

_____

_____

_____

Day 2: Which affirmation speaks loudest to you? Why?

_____

_____

_____

Day 3: In what ways have you already focused on that one?

_____

_____

_____

Day 4: Which affirmation is your biggest challenge? Why?

_____

_____

_____

Day 5: What can you do to make it easier to believe?

_____

_____

_____

Day 6: How do you feel about these affirmations now?

_____

_____

_____

Day 7: Write your own "I believe I am..." affirmation.

_____

_____

WEEK 16

"I will stop..."

Say these affirmations aloud every day.

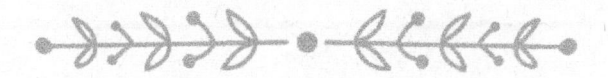

I will stop chasing potential.

I will stop putting my trust in empty promises.

I will stop painting over another's true colors.

I will stop trying to force something that isn't there.

I will stop investing in those not invested in me.

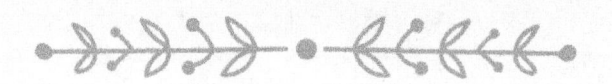

Write one of the affirmations each night before bed.

Day

1 _____

2 _____

3 _____

4 _____

5 _____

6 _____

7 _____

THOUGHT EXERCISE

Day 1: How does admitting your bad habits make you feel?

_____

_____

_____

_____

Day 2: Which affirmation speaks loudest to you? Why?

_____

_____

_____

_____

Day 3: In what ways have you already focused on that one?

_____

_____

_____

_____

Day 4: Which affirmation is your biggest challenge? Why?

_____

_____

_____

_____

Day 5: What can you do to make it easier to believe?

_____

_____

_____

_____

Day 6: How do you feel about the affirmations now?

_____

_____

_____

Day 7: Write your own "I will stop…" affirmation.

_____

_____

WEEK 17

"I prioritize..."

Say these affirmations aloud every day.

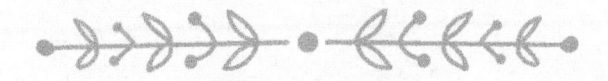

I prioritize
my needs.

I prioritize
my wants.

I prioritize
my mental health.

I prioritize
a relationship with myself.

I prioritize
my spiritual health.

Write one of the affirmations each night before bed.

Day

1 _____
_____

2 _____
_____

3 _____
_____

4 _____
_____

5 _____
_____

6 _____
_____

7 _____
_____

THOUGHT EXERCISE

Day 1: What does prioritizing mean to you in this case?

_____

_____

_____

Day 2: Which affirmation speaks loudest to you? Why?

_____

_____

_____

Day 3: In what ways have you already focused on that one?

_____

_____

_____

Day 4: Which affirmation is your biggest challenge? Why?

_____

_____

_____

_____

Day 5: What can you do to make it easier to believe?

_____

_____

_____

_____

Day 6: How do you feel about these affirmations now?

_____

_____

_____

_____

Day 7: Write your own "I prioritize..." affirmation.

_____

_____

WEEK 18

"I will conquer..."

Say these affirmations aloud every day.

I will conquer
my insecurities.

I will conquer
my fear.

I will conquer
my trauma.

I will conquer
the things in my life that keep
me from being the best healed
version of myself.

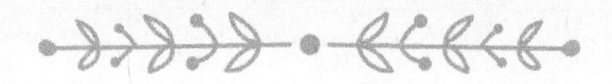

Write one of the affirmations each night before bed.

Day

1 _____
_____

2 _____
_____

3 _____
_____

4 _____
_____

5 _____
_____

6 _____
_____

7 _____
_____

THOUGHT EXERCISE

Day 1: What does conquering mean to you in this case?

_____

_____

_____

_____

Day 2: Which affirmation speaks loudest to you? Why?

_____

_____

_____

_____

Day 3: In what ways have you already focused on that one?

_____

_____

_____

_____

Day 4: Which affirmation is your biggest challenge? Why?

_____
_____
_____
_____

Day 5: What can you do to make it easier to believe?

_____
_____
_____
_____

Day 6: How do you feel about these affirmations now?

_____
_____
_____
_____

Day 7: Write your own "I will conquer..." affirmation.

_____
_____

WEEK 19

"I am open to..."

Say these affirmations aloud every day.

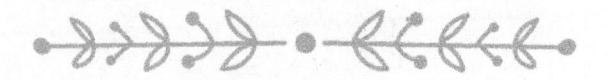

I am open to
good conversations.

I am open to
new friendships and beautiful
connections.

I am open to
new opportunities and new interests.

I am open to
promising relationships.

I am open to new love.

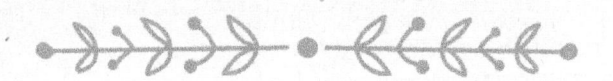

Write one of the affirmations each night before bed.

Day

1 _____
_____

2 _____
_____

3 _____
_____

4 _____
_____

5 _____
_____

6 _____
_____

7 _____
_____

THOUGHT EXERCISE

Day 1: What does being open mean to you in this case?

_____

_____

_____

_____

Day 2: Which affirmation speaks loudest to you? Why?

_____

_____

_____

_____

Day 3: In what ways have you already focused on that one?

_____

_____

_____

_____

Day 4: Which affirmation is your biggest challenge? Why?

_____

_____

_____

_____

Day 5: What can you do to make it easier to believe?

_____

_____

_____

_____

Day 6: How do you feel about these affirmations now?

_____

_____

_____

Day 7: Write your own "I am open to..." affirmation.

_____

_____

WEEK 20

"I deserve..."

Say these affirmations aloud every day.

I deserve
a relationship that will add
more to me than take.

I deserve
a partner that will value me.

I deserve
the good things life has for me.

I deserve
to be accepted for who I am.

I deserve
happiness, joy, and safety.

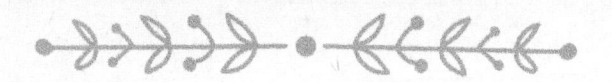

Write one of the affirmations each night before bed.

Day

1 _____
_____

2 _____
_____

3 _____
_____

4 _____
_____

5 _____
_____

6 _____
_____

7 _____
_____

THOUGHT EXERCISE

Day 1: How do you feel about declaring your wants/needs?

_____
_____
_____
_____

Day 2: Which affirmation speaks loudest to you? Why?

_____
_____
_____
_____

Day 3: In what ways have you already focused on that one?

_____
_____
_____
_____

Day 4: Which affirmation is your biggest challenge? Why?

_____

_____

_____

_____

Day 5: What can you do to make it easier to believe?

_____

_____

_____

_____

Day 6: How do you feel about these affirmations now?

_____

_____

_____

Day 7: Write your own "I deserve..." affirmation.

_____

_____

WEEK 21

"I will..."

Say these affirmations aloud every day.

I will heal and
grow at my own pace.

I will make adjustments
when the timing is
right for me.

I will move
the way I need to move.

I will listen to
and trust myself.

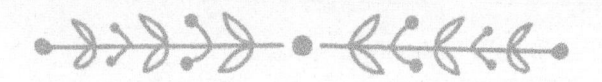

Write one of the affirmations each night before bed.

Day

1 _____

2 _____

3 _____

4 _____

5 _____

6 _____

7 _____

THOUGHT EXERCISE

Day 1: How do you feel about declaring your growth?

_____
_____
_____
_____

Day 2: Which affirmation speaks loudest to you? Why?

_____
_____
_____
_____

Day 3: In what ways have you already focused on that one?

_____
_____
_____
_____

Day 4: Which affirmation is your biggest challenge? Why?

_____

_____

_____

_____

Day 5: What can you do to make it easier to believe?

_____

_____

_____

_____

Day 6: How do you feel about these affirmations now?

_____

_____

_____

_____

Day 7: Write your own "I will..." affirmation.

_____

_____

WEEK 22

"I am done..."

Say these affirmations aloud every day.

I am done holding on to
what I should let go.

I am done keeping the door
of my heart open for those who
don't want to stay.

I am done letting others define me.

I am done sacrificing
more than I should for people
who sacrifice nothing for me.

I am done crossing oceans
for the wrong people.

Write one of the affirmations each night before bed.

Day

1

2

3

4

5

6

7

THOUGHT EXERCISE

Day 1: What does being "done" mean to you in this case?

_____

_____

_____

_____

Day 2: Which affirmation speaks loudest to you? Why?

_____

_____

_____

_____

Day 3: In what ways have you already focused on that one?

_____

_____

_____

_____

Day 4: Which affirmation is your biggest challenge? Why?

_____
_____
_____
_____

Day 5: What can you do to make it easier to believe?

_____
_____
_____
_____

Day 6: How do you feel about these affirmations now?

_____
_____
_____

Day 7: Write your own "I am done..." affirmation.

_____
_____

WEEK 23

"I am letting go..."

Say these affirmations aloud every day.

I am letting go of
what hurt me.

I am letting go of
who hurt me.

I am letting go of what doesn't
belong in my future.

I am letting go of who doesn't
belong in my future.

I am letting go of those who only
know to hold me back.

Write one of the affirmations each night before bed.

Day

1 _____
  _____

2 _____
  _____

3 _____
  _____

4 _____
  _____

5 _____
  _____

6 _____
  _____

7 _____
  _____

THOUGHT EXERCISE

Day 1: What does "letting go" mean to you in this case?

_____

_____

_____

_____

Day 2: Which affirmation speaks loudest to you? Why?

_____

_____

_____

_____

Day 3: In what ways have you already focused on that one?

_____

_____

_____

_____

Day 4: Which affirmation is your biggest challenge? Why?

_____

_____

_____

_____

Day 5: What can you do to make it easier to believe?

_____

_____

_____

_____

Day 6: How do you feel about these affirmations now?

_____

_____

Day 7: Write your own "I am letting go of..." affirmation.

_____

_____

WEEK 24

"I am ready to..."

Say these affirmations aloud every day.

I am ready to
leave the past behind.

I am ready to
leave unhealthy habits behind.

I am ready to
leave unproductive
friendships behind.

I am ready to
leave toxic beliefs behind.

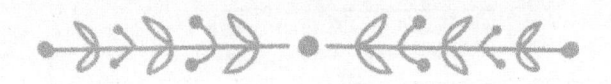

Write one of the affirmations each night before bed.

Day

1
_____
_____

2
_____
_____

3
_____
_____

4
_____
_____

5
_____
_____

6
_____
_____

7
_____
_____

THOUGHT EXERCISE

Day 1: Do you feel ready to make changes? Why? Why not?

_____

_____

_____

_____

Day 2: Which affirmation speaks loudest to you? Why?

_____

_____

_____

_____

Day 3: In what ways have you already focused on that one?

_____

_____

_____

_____

Day 4: Which affirmation is your biggest challenge? Why?

_____
_____
_____

Day 5: What can you do to make it easier to believe?

_____
_____
_____

Day 6: How do you feel about these affirmations now?

_____
_____
_____

Day 7: Write your own "I am ready to…" affirmation.

_____
_____

WEEK 25
"I give myself permission to..."

Say these affirmations aloud every day.

I give myself permission to
laugh without restraint.

I give myself permission to
smile again without caring about
my insecurities.

I give myself permission to
be truly happy in my own skin.

I give myself permission to
live boldly on my own terms.

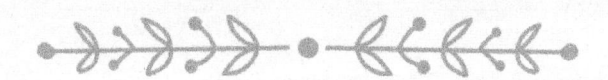

Write one of the affirmations each night before bed.

Day

1 _____

2 _____

3 _____

4 _____

5 _____

6 _____

7 _____

THOUGHT EXERCISE

Day 1: What does giving yourself "permission" mean to you in this case?

_____
_____
_____
_____

Day 2: Which affirmation speaks loudest to you? Why?

_____
_____
_____
_____

Day 3: In what ways have you already focused on that one?

_____
_____
_____
_____

Day 4: Which affirmation is your biggest challenge? Why?

_____
_____
_____
_____

Day 5: What can you do to make it easier to believe?

_____
_____
_____
_____

Day 6: How do you feel about the affirmations now?

_____
_____
_____

Day 7: Write your own "I give myself permission..." affirmation.

_____
_____

WEEK 26

"I will be patient..."

Say these affirmations aloud every day.

I will be patient
because my best life is worth
waiting for and I can see it clearly.

I will be patient
because healing takes time
and I am worth it.

I will be patient
because what is for me
will find its way to me.

I will be patient
because who is for me
will find their way into my life.

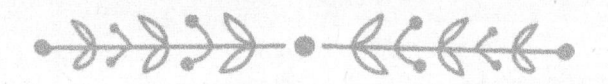

Write one of the affirmations each night before bed.

Day

1 _____

2 _____

3 _____

4 _____

5 _____

6 _____

7 _____

THOUGHT EXERCISE

Day 1: What does patience mean to you in this case?

_____

_____

_____

_____

Day 2: Which affirmation speaks loudest to you? Why?

_____

_____

_____

_____

Day 3: In what ways have you already focused on that one?

_____

_____

_____

_____

Day 4: Which affirmation is your biggest challenge? Why?

_____

_____

_____

Day 5: What can you do to make it easier to believe?

_____

_____

_____

Day 6: How do you feel about the affirmations now?

_____

_____

_____

Day 7: Write your own "I will be patient..." affirmation.

_____

_____

You made it through.
YOU. DID. IT.
I am so proud of you!
I hope this book and these affirmations and thought exercises made a world of a difference for you.

Please, don't hesitate to return back to page one and do this all over again. Keep incorporating affirmations into your life, they are powerful tools.

The best of luck to you.

Pierre Alex Jeanty, most widely known for his international best sellers *HER* & *HER Vol.2*, is a Haitian-American author, publisher, life coach, and entrepreneur. Often approached for relationship advice and dealing with the same issues himself, Pierre found a passion for writing on the topics of dating, love, and relationships. After leaving his 9-to-5 in 2014 to become a full-time relationship blogger, Pierre released his first book *Unspoken Feelings of a Gentleman* which quickly rocketed to success.

Since then, he's maintained a balance between writing self-help and writing poetry. He also writes for men and women, which led to him to launch the HER series in 2017. Pierre's focus is to share his own love journey and lessons from his past, with the hope that it inspires men to become better, and to be a voice of hope to women who have lost faith in good men.

Pierre currently resides with his family in southwest Florida where he operates as the founder of Jeanius Publishing, a publishing company dedicated to helping authors. Pierre also occasionally travels as a speaker and is the host of "The REALationship Therapy" podcast with his wife, Natalie Jeanty.

You can connect with Pierre on these platforms:

@Pierrejeanty

Pierre Alex Jeanty

@PierreAJeanty

Other books by Pierre

Best Sellers

HER.

HER Vol. 2

HIM.

Ashes of Her Love

Unspoken Feelings of a Gentleman

To the Women I Once Loved

Apologies That Never Came

Other Books

Really Moving On

Her. Guided Journal

Unspoken Feelings of a Gentleman 2

In Love With You

Heal. Grow. Love.

Sparking Her Own Flame

Loving Me Right

Watering Your Soil

Free Downloads

Watering Your Soil
Download at www.wateringyoursoil.com